MW00949249

This Notebook Belongs To :

[illegible]

[illegible] [illegible]

Thank you for your purchase.

If you are happy with your book, please take a minute to leave a positive review.

Made in the USA
Monee, IL
25 January 2023

26229455R10056